THE WISDOM ORACLE

An Aid to Accessing Your Inner Wisdom

Featuring

The Ancient Wisdom of Proverbs

And

The Totem Animal Messengers of The Great Spirit

Copyright © James McQuitty 2013

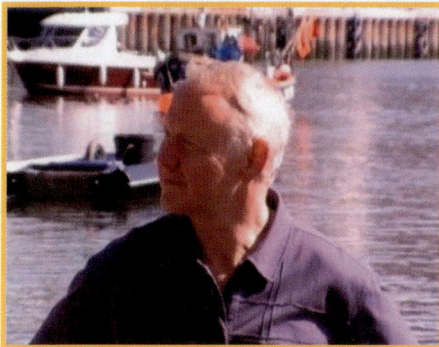

www.jamesmcquitty.com

A Philosophical Note

At a deeper or subconscious level you have far greater understanding than you might realise. The real you, the spirit that you truly *are* understands your purpose for incarnation and the pathways that you should tread.

A Note about the Proverbs

With exception to a few more modern additions, a number of the proverbs contained in this book date back hundreds of years, when the use of masculine phrasing was more in vogue. In most such cases I have slightly amended the phrasing to a neutral arrangement.

Introduction

I have been writing spiritual literature since 1993; having originally started in response to the suggestion of a spirit guide.

My writing mission has mostly been one of study and discerning truth from fantasy. Then to put what I learn, and sometimes this is intuitive, an inner knowing or sudden revelation, into understandable terms, this I have endeavoured to do with each of my books.

In a sense *this* book *is* the result of revelation–not directly from the Great Spirit–but because it was inspired by a Chinese spirit guide called *Sun Lee*. In a personal message through a medium I was told that he was to help me write a book, and the inspiration to construct this oracle followed. I hope you find it worthy and of value as an aid to accessing your own inner or higher self wisdom–which you undoubtedly possess.

Foreword

Consulting any oracle can help you to access your inner or higher self wisdom, your connection to divinity. In this book proverbs and secondly totem animals are used to open the mind to greater self-awareness. Proverbs are short, pithy, traditional sayings in common use; they reflect the wisdom of the people; hence the book title. Totem animals are messengers of The Great Spirit that through visions (including meditation or contemplation) and dreams attempt to guide you along your pathway.

This oracle is an aid to self-reflective guidance. It is not a form of divination, so you will not find answers that say yes or no or that you will embark upon a great romance, live happily to a healthy old age, or become rich or famous. Rather, you will be guided to look more deeply at self, for whatever reading is drawn to you (and I suggest you use two dice to determine this) will cast a reflection of the inner or real you, and who knows self better than self. In this way they act as a catalyst to self-realisation, helping to bring to a conscious level what at a deeper level you already know. How, in response to this greater awareness you choose to act, is still a matter of your own freewill choice.

Strictly speaking it is unnecessary for you to read each proverb, totem animal and following reading before attempting consultation, for their order will be registered in the universal unconscious mind to which we all connect. Principally, they are intended for single use, to assist guidance on one concern at a time. However, more experienced readers and those who feel so inclined may wish to indulge themselves in the equivalent of spread formations, such as first selection referring to the past, the next to the present time, and a third to suggest a possible future situation.

I would recommend that you consult them with reverence, preferably after a prayer for guidance and illumination, for such an act itself attracts higher guidance. It is a fact that sacred requests are always answered; not necessarily in the way in which on a conscious level we might wish, but answered in a way that best facilitates personal spiritual growth. You may of course consult them for fun if you so wish, but this will most likely bring an equally fun result, for in many respects they will act as a mirror.

There are many and varied ways in which the proverbs and totem animals contained within can resonate within your being, physically, emotionally, mentally and spiritually. When through a throw of the dice you make a selection its message might immediately make sense to you so that a pathway to follow or a course of action to take becomes clear to you. I would suggest contemplation upon the selected proverb as a first focal point, however, using a mental image of the totem animal and concentration upon this will help those readers who prefer a mental image, and for this reason (because the key to the mind for one person can be different from that of another) they are included. If nothing comes to mind you can either meditate or contemplate upon the proverb or totem animal you receive or leave the matter to rest and perhaps some hours later, or in a dream, it is likely that some meaning will come to you. The delay is because the subconscious or higher self is a level of mind that few find easy to consult at will; remember that *Patience is a virtue*. When thoughts do come quickly it is likely that the response to self was closer to the surface or conscious mind.

This oracle should be consulted in neutral fashion; that is to say, you should seek guidance upon a subject rather than ask a specific question. Phrasing should therefore be something like, *I seek guidance upon romance,* or, *I seek guidance in relation to my health, finances, spirituality, (or whatever).* If seeking for another person you should first obtain their permission, then include their name in your request.

Reading Interpretations

The readings that follow each of the proverbs and totem animals are for guidance *only*. They are interpretations that sprang to *my* mind while in quiet contemplation at the time of drafting. Your thoughts will undoubtedly differ because we are all different and each on our own pathways of discovery and growth, so whether they differ greatly or just a little it is recommended, indeed important, that you follow your own feelings.

To give yourself every chance of finding your own inner guidance, I suggest that you seek inwardly for your own intuitive interpretations before reading (or re-reading) my thoughts. This will allow your own thoughts to formulate and strike an inner cord before comparison.

Using Dice for Selection

It is not essential to use dice for selection, you may prefer to simply open the book to a random page and read this. However, I believe you will find it more rewarding to use two different coloured dice, and the book is scripted with this in mind. You can then designate one dice as the first and the other the second digit. (Alternatively, you may simply use one dice and throw it twice!).

With exception to the one recommendation already made, to first say a prayer for guidance, there are no rituals or rules to follow in throwing your dice. You can throw straight from your hands or use a tumbler, whichever method you prefer.

You do need a flat surface of adequate size so that the dice do not easily roll off (if either should fall I would recommend throwing both again). The readings follow in straightforward order, first dice and second dice numbers. I hope you have fun and find inspiration.

1 & 1

Know Thyself

The Owl - The Spirit of Wisdom

This proverb suggests that you may need to look deep within, at your true feelings, your true motives and desires to check whether they are worthy of the spirit you are. Nobody can know self completely, it is impossible, but connecting with the core of your own being is what this encourages. This is the ultimate call; it is perhaps the most significant throw of the dice possible-the call to know yourself. It is an appeal for courage, commitment and most importantly honesty; encouraging you to face your true self, your true aspirations, to know self and crucially to be true to self. Yet, as another proverb says, *'To err is human.'* So do not be too critical with yourself if you find shortcomings, for we all have them. If we did not, we would have no need of this incarnation. Another proverb says, *'Experience is the mother of wisdom,'* but this does not come overnight, it is a long-haul assignment of the soul.

The Owl, the spirit of wisdom, is associated with this proverb. It is a wise observation to recognise your own faults and weaknesses, but this alone does not make one wise. Wisdom is to act upon what is found in a positive, constructive and loving way.

Cosmically, we are multi-dimensional beings operating on more than one level of consciousness at a time whether we realise so or not. We are aspects of divinity, aspects of each other. We are individualised aspects of our soul group, which is an aspect of a larger group, which itself is an aspect of a still larger group into infinity, until, by the spiritual law of divine oneness, all is one.

Live And Let Live

The Dove – The Spirit of Peace and Love

This proverb reminds you that you have the right to live as you see fit; if necessary, to stand up for yourself and reclaim your right to personal expression. While it may also be a call to remind you of the fact that others also have this right, and to loosen any undue restrictions you may be tempted to impose. Another proverb says, '*The course of true love never did run smooth*,' and this reminds us that in order to avoid despondency we must, '*Live and let live.*'

Linked with this proverb is the spirit of peace and love in the form of the Dove. It says that like the Dove, on occasions we all have to spread our wings and fly. To feel the free flowing air beneath us as we move towards a destination, new or familiar, eventually to land and set our feet upon the ground. Always we will be free spirits and our imaginations can roam far and wide, yet we need to remain somewhat rational, so that we do not float away into mystical realms of fantasy, for in physical terms we must remain creatures of the earth. Spiritual law teaches us that charity and goodwill, with a capacity to be lenient in judging others, is a virtue.

There is a time to be born and a time to return home (to spirit). There, freedom to live how one chooses, subject to what has been earned, is enjoyed. On earth there can be physical and financial restrictions, but there is nothing stopping us from at least working towards our goals and hopefully bringing some to fruition. We should all strive to live our own lives in the way that we intuitively feel is best while giving others the same respect and courtesy.

1 & 3

Those Who Make No Mistakes, Make Nothing

The Monkey - The Spirit of Curiosity

The message behind this proverb encourages you to try your hardest to succeed. Even when it seems impossible the effort may well set in motion a causation to bring success or satisfaction. It may also be saying that the very act of attempt is virtuous and brings its own reward. The cosmos loves one who tries, you may be disappointed time and time again, but rewards so often come to those who have repeatedly striven to realise their dreams. Even when all may seem against you, as another proverb says, *'April showers bring forth May flowers.'*

Associated with this proverb is the Monkey, the spirit of curiosity. Encouraging you to experience all that comes before you. To be like the Monkey who plays, experiments, tests and tastes, yet most of all strives to enjoy the experience. He swings on the rope without questioning whether it is strong enough to bear his weight; those who through fear refuse to trust or live life to the full miss so much of the fun.

Mistakes in all walks and avenues of life are natural, for none of us is perfect, if we were we would have no need of this incarnation. Life is a succession of mistakes from which we learn and grow. The biggest mistake anyone can make is to fear and risk nothing, for this is stagnation. Those who risk nothing gain nothing. So continue to strive, to risk (without harm to others), for in going forward you ultimately advance, not always in physical terms, but always in spiritual progression.

1 & 4

Love Will Find A Way

*The Dolphin – The Spirit of
Happiness and Harmony*

Love is a two-way power, this proverb indicates that you should give and be open to receive, even if the circumstances currently prevailing seem a hindrance, a way will be found. Love is the infinite-ultimate power of creation. We can never grasp the totality of this upon the physical plane because love descends through the dimensions and spheres to our own level of consciousness and this effectively limits it. Yet to our own capacity to experience, it always finds a way.

The spirit of happiness and harmony in the form of the delightful Dolphin is associated with this proverb. Many have swum in the sea and been blessed by the healing energies that come as they encounter this happy creature. He (or she) brings a balancing effect to their energies. This is natural love, the emotional harmonising of unconditional love given freely, one form to another, or for all. A touch of the utopia that can be, that one day we will all find, you are reminded that you are not excluded or forgotten.

Love is a free commodity, it costs nothing to give and you may freely receive it. It is a power that once you give surely you will receive (time in this equation being indeterminable) as the great law of cause and effect fulfils itself so that love begets love and those who project happiness and joy attract equally likeminded souls. In time all receive what they deserve, and love will find a way, it has to, for it is the power of creation.

1 & 5

Actions Speak Louder Than Words

The Elephant - The Spirit of Kindness, Sacrifice and Service

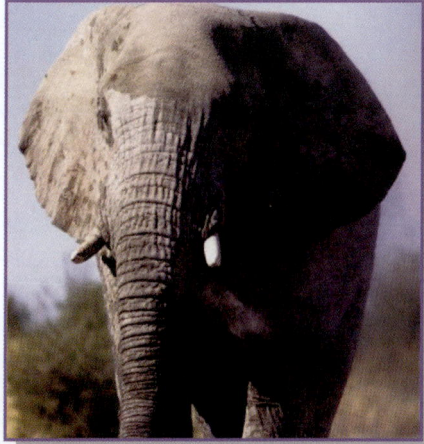

This proverb counsels action. It suggests that you have pondered or spoken of what is on your mind, but now it is time for action, to do rather than to say. Whether this is to go ahead or to conclude a matter only you, according to how you feel, can decide. Either way, it may well be time to make a decision and to act according to it. As another proverb that is worth remembering says, '*There is great difference between word and deed.*'

The Elephant, the spirit of kindness, sacrifice and service, is linked with this proverb. He (or she) is a gentle giant who gives and responds most admirably to acts of appreciation, care, attention, respect and love. Those who can say that their actions and responses and those of people around them are of equal measure can be congratulated for their own behaviour and on their choice of friends. Those who cannot, have something to work at.

In the process of spiritual advancement there is a time to rest and a time to act. The spiritual law of action can require a change in behaviour. Contemplation to consider the likely outcome and consequences of your actions before they are undertaken is wisdom in action. Kindness can be expressed in many ways, a simple thank you, by showing respect, as well as by actions.

None Knows the Weight of Another's Burden

The Wolf - The Spirit of the Pathfinder and Knowledge

This proverb can be viewed in two ways. First, if what you seek guidance upon involves another person, it urges you to look more closely at all that might be weighing them down and that this may be more than you realise. Second, if it concerns yourself only, are there burdens weighing you down which others do not see or appreciate? Either way, to move forward in the way you seek, it would be advisable to first alleviate some (or all) of the burdens. Then, with a lighter load to bear you (or they) can more easily move forward towards your dreams. Another proverb says, '*It is comparison that makes people happy or miserable*,' to be happy seek the pathway that satisfies your soul urge.

Linked with this proverb is the spirit of the pathfinder and knowledge in the form of the Wolf. The Wolf understands the wild; often he has stood upon a mountaintop and looked down to observe all that is happening below. Sometimes greater knowledge must be sought to reveal the truth behind any situation. Does the Wolf encourage you to do likewise?

In the spiritual sense we should never judge others. For we rarely know the full extent of what has happened to shape their character and life. Damage to the foundations of the tallest building can cause it to collapse. Also, the learning opportunities we each face as life unfolds can for each of us be at vastly different points on the pathway of eternal progression. Compassion is a spiritual virtue to be admired, to give unconditional love, to think before speaking, to listen, not judge.

2 & 1

Rome Was Not Built In a Day

The Dog - The Spirit of Dedication and Loyalty

This proverb encourages patience, for little of worth can be achieved quickly. It takes time and effort to build anything that you would wish to be long lasting, whether physical, emotional, mental or spiritual in nature. As another proverb says, '*There is no good building without good foundations.*' So it says, do not rush, instead contemplate, evaluate, ponder for a while to weigh the pros and cons then, when more sure of the desired outcome, lay the foundations and begin.

Associated with this proverb is the Dog, symbolising the spirit of dedication and loyalty. Life constantly requires degrees of dedication if we are to accomplish anything of value. Loyalty can take many forms, to a cause, a friend, a loved one, and indeed to the inner calling of the spirit. The dog gives these things and love too; those who can follow this example are the better person for doing so.

Following this sojourn on the earth plane others do not judge us for our lifetimes, but we do build our own futures. What has gone we cannot change, although we can wherever necessary attempt restitution. We are constantly involved in a long-haul spiritual building project during which we can show patience with self and others as we strive to build a better self. But most important is to be true to inner feelings.

*The Greatest Wealth
Is Contentment with a Little*

*The Robin - The Spirit of
Service, Joy and Light*

This proverb asks you to sit back and contemplate. For although you may wish for more in your seeking, it may be that you also have much with which to be satisfied. Perhaps you should be a little more contented with your lot, for is this not greater than many enjoy? It says, be appreciative, relax and consider all the positives you enjoy. There is another proverb worth remembering that says, '*Blessed are they who expect nothing, for they shall never be disappointed.*' In other words seek needs and try not to covet too many wants.

The spirit of service, joy and light in the form of the Robin is associated with this proverb. The Robin serves as it builds its nest then feeds and cares for her young, while it freely delights us with song. So she encourages you to do likewise and in this way to find joy, light and the wealth of pleasure that comes to a contented soul. Contentment can also come in giving, in service to people, animals, the environment and in so many other ways.

To be unselfish, openhearted and generous of spirit is a virtue of great merit that by the spiritual law of attraction will reap rewards. The law teaches us that according to how we are on the inside (the real person) we draw to ourselves in this life and the next. The light of the spirit is in the aura of the person, herein shines the wealth of the soul.

Never Put Off Till Tomorrow What May Be Done Today

The Badger - The Spirit of Courage

This proverb suggests that there is something you should have done, but for whatever reason you have delayed or hesitated over proceeding. If so this is your call to delay no longer, to get on and do it. You will undoubtedly find, as so often is the case that once faced and experienced you will wonder why you ever dilly-dallied in the first place. Another proverb you may wish to consider is, '*Sooner begun, sooner done.*' Both encourage you to be bold, brave and have no fear for a bright tomorrow will always follow.

The Badger, the spirit of courage, is linked with this proverb. This encourages you to keep faith with yourself. Hard work may be necessary but because of this, when completed, it will give you greater satisfaction than if it came easy. This will enable you to recognise your worth, and you can justifiably claim your due reward.

Lifetime after lifetime we are confronted with challenges to experience; from these we (hopefully) move forward as more enlightened beings. It is in this way that we learn, develop and grow. The adversities of life and how we deal with them are necessary experiences. We would naturally prefer experiences of love and joy, but in many ways these are heightened by the less than pleasurable, for these make the happier times seem that much more rewarding and tangible to us. Developing greater courage, not reckless dare devil courage, but the courage to stay calm and where necessary face opposition fairly, with higher-self guidance, is a spiritual virtue.

Every Oak Has Been an Acorn

The Rabbit – The Spirit of Evolution and Fertility

This proverb indicates that which you seek guidance upon, no matter if others consider it a small matter, has within the potential to develop and grow into something more substantial. This most likely is a call to go for it, and to expect a pleasing outcome. For as another proverb says, *'From small beginnings come great things.'* Things may not happen overnight, they may take time to reach full potential, but like the oak they will have great strength and the potential to establish deep and meaningful roots. Every idea, plan, project, good deed, at its outset has been an acorn, a thought that has formulated then been acted upon.

Linked with this proverb is the spirit of evolution and fertility, in the form of the Rabbit. Encouraging you to move forward, to let your fertile imagination expand and to let your thoughts evolve to full potential. It may also be a time to embark upon a new adventure.

Nature herself is never at a standstill, even when unseen by the human eye, for at a cellular or microscopic level activity abounds. Physical evolution begins at this level and over aeons of time progresses to more complex and advanced life forms. The summit form upon earth is the human being. Spirit evolution through form experience follows this pathway of progression as we overcome and master tests in our evolutionary pathway.

2 & 5

To Put the Cat among the Pigeons

The Tiger - The Spirit of Energy, Action and Freedom

This proverb signals a need to stir things up and see what happens. Feathers may fly, but sometimes it serves no purpose to hold back, for some people only take note when confronted head-on. Remember what another proverb says, *'All are not saints that go to church.'* By taking action now, you can reveal the truth and reclaim your independence.

Associated with this proverb is the Tiger, symbolising the spirit of energy, action and freedom. The Tiger can give you the energy and the drive to move forward in your actions. At the same time it is important that you retain your sense of freedom, whether literally or of thought. This big cat can be a solitary creature, yet as he follows his natural instincts, his nature, he has his moments. At times we must all do likewise, and follow our inner direction.

Many famous persons (including mediums) have experienced controversy and difficult times in their life. Many have passed through years of struggle, with little to inspire them. Yet, from one moment of inspiration, one catalyst or realisation of self-worth, they have progressed to become much appreciated (on Earth and in spirit) for the love they have given to the world. The motive behind any action is always of paramount importance, if it is just, never be afraid to proceed.

Hitch Your Wagon to a Star

The Snake - The Spirit of Transformation

This proverb encourages you to follow your dreams. To go for what you most want to do. Whether it is of a physical, emotional, mental or spiritual nature, dreams are our inspiration to go forward. You may have to be brave, a reason many leave their dreams unfulfilled. You are encouraged not to do likewise, not to give way to fear of failure or embarrassment, but to set your vision high and follow the guiding light of your inner star, your inner vision. Another proverb that inspires says, *'Life is a pilgrimage,'* why not make yours a quest to hitch onto the brightest star?

The spirit of transformation in the form of the Snake is associated with this proverb. This symbolises the shedding of one skin (the past?) to reveal the new (the inner you?). It can also signify a breakthrough in some form. Perhaps the freeing of the spirit from the mundane or the limitations that can so often hold us back from the fulfilment of dreams?

Higher guidance often comes in dreams or flashes of inspiration in sleep or waking state. Often it is in symbolic imagery, which can be spirit telepathy and equivalent of sign language. Just as traffic signs often show symbols we can understand your dreams try to do likewise. They can mean, stop, go, or ponder and consider and much more, and it is in this way that higher guidance attempts to inspire, encourage and clearly focus your mind and emotions.

3 & 1

A Stitch in Time Saves Nine

The Hummingbird - The Spirit of Joy, Health and Love

This proverb signifies that now may be a good time to bring something out into the open. That any differences would benefit by discussion, so that relationships or circles of friends do not fall apart. You are encouraged, as another proverb says, '*To take the Bull by the horns*;' for misunderstandings have caused the downfall of friendships and nations alike. An early repair, remedial action, can avoid so much grief.

The spirit of joy, health and love in the form of the beautiful Hummingbird is linked with this proverb. This symbolises a blessing and heralds the coming of better times, perhaps to make up for all that has gone before. It also encourages healing, particularly self-healing, and love makes this more possible than anything else, for it is the power of creation.

The universe asks very little in return for its existence. It echoes to us through the vibrations of life wishing and hoping that we could live in harmony with it, with creation. With infinite patience it observes our struggle to find the joy of love that has always been at our core. The cosmos comes from love, is love in form, it is the fabric of life that will never tear. Those who can attune themselves can find eternal joy, self-love and respect, and perfection in all things.

3 & 2

Do As You Would Be Done By

The Deer - The Spirit of Compassion

This proverb calls upon you to follow a pathway of compassion. For who amongst us is so perfect that we have not made mistakes. It says, '*If you do not wish to be judged, do not judge others.*' Equally, this can all be applied to self. So be fair and compassionate to yourself. The past is the past, we need not forget all that is gone for we learn from it, but where necessary we can forgive self and others. As you move forward in life it may well be worth remembering another proverb that says, '*It is better to do well than to say well.*'

Linked with this proverb is The Deer, the spirit of compassion. This encourages growth in self, a spiritual advancement, whilst it can also encompass a rebirth, the arrival of the *new* you. The revealing of your true inner feelings made manifest for all to see and embrace. It says, give love by showing compassion, see the good (the God) in all and help draw this to the surface, as you would wish for yourself. It is there, within all forms, even the seemingly lowest, recognise it, embrace it and encourage it.

Those who climb the mountain find areas of gentle incline before they face the peak. So it is with life, we can settle for the easier pathway, or we can progress to the tougher peaks of compassion and forgiveness. If we give unconditional love and let compassion replace judgement our advancement can indeed be wondrous.

3 & 3

The Proof Of The Pudding
Is In the Eating

The Hawk - The Spirit of
Observation

At issue with this proverb is a need to accept what is becoming obvious to you. Proof comes in many ways, in the clear and undeniable that is personally witnessed, in the sworn testimony of others as used in the law courts, *beyond reasonable doubt*, in repeated actions or behaviour. It may also come as a bolt of lightning that strikes at the heart as a sure and certain knowing. Equally this may be a call to be in possession of all the facts before you act. To test or try out your theory or belief before you move forward. Another proverb you may need to ponder says, '*Fair words and foul deeds cheat the wise as well as the fools.*'

Associated with this proverb is the spirit of observation in the form of the Hawk. The Hawk encourages you to see the pathway, the gateway or opening when it presents itself to you. It urges you to be focused, to keep your eyes open, for at times you may have seen only what you or others wanted you to see, rather than what is truly there, so do stay alert. In doing so you will find what you need.

Seeking for proof is the cornerstone of commonsense. It is what every good philosopher and scientist does. Beliefs are torn to shreds as new replace old, whereas proof is eternal and undeniable. Those who blindly swallow beliefs are invariably disappointed. Proof is a solid foundation, and the best proof comes through personal experience.

A Leap in the Dark

The Unicorn - The Spirit of Faith and Hope

Do you have the courage, the faith perhaps, to take a leap in the dark? For this proverb does counsel you to once again take the plunge into the unknown. We have all done so before; indeed we can never be totally sure how any experience will unfold. So you are encouraged to be bold, to go for what you feel you would like, ultimately you will be glad that you did. For whether or not things progress as you might wish, you will learn from the experience; as another proverb says, '*All roads lead to Rome.*'

The Unicorn, the spirit of faith and hope, is associated with this proverb. This suggests it may be a good time for you to harvest what in the past you have sown. To receive the rewards that by your own efforts, and those with which you have kept faith, manifest in some delightful way. At present you may remain for a little longer in the dark, but very soon you will be carried away on the back of your friendly companion to new and brighter horizons, so trust and be ready to move forward.

We all take a leap in the dark when we are born. We return with an experience plan, a blueprint for life, although consciously we do not recollect it, so we have to trust that enough of our spiritual light will shine through to illuminate our pathway. To recognise that there is a purpose in all things and that expectations will be fulfilled, to believe and hang on to dreams.

3 & 5

Walk the Walk

The Puma - The Spirit of Grace and Silent Power

This proverb suggests that the time has come for you to act upon the knowledge you already possess. It is perhaps time for you to stand up and be counted, to do rather than to say, or to make your feelings known. You are encouraged to be true to self. To follow the pathway, take action, or respond according to your true feelings or inner guidance. As another proverb says, '*One must draw the line somewhere,*' and yours should be clear enough for you to see.

The spirit of grace and silent power in the form of the Puma is linked with this proverb. The Puma is the companion of the shaman on journeys to the spirit realms. Symbolising vision, insight and perhaps even an initiation into something grander than you might dare to dream. To gain entry or pass the test, to establish your worth, you must at all times and in all situations be willing to *walk the walk*. Not by screaming and shouting, but by example, so that your grace and silent power can likewise attract and lead others to the pathway.

Globally, it can be said that the time to walk the walk has arrived. Nations are being called upon to act most urgently on environmental issues rather than continually *talk the talk*, because time waits for no one. Spiritually, we must walk the walk to progress to higher spiritual realms. The silent power of good loving thoughts produces positive energies in our own lives and helps transmute world energy towards balanced harmony.

3 & 6

Every Cloud Has a Silver Lining

The Bee - The Spirit of Generosity and Labour

This proverb suggests that whatever situation you currently find yourself in, and however it is affecting your life, it is a process of clearing or preparation so that new growth may follow. Nature does this in numerous ways, some at first glance seem cruel and unfair, but old invariably gives way to new. What seems bad luck to one is good fortune to another. Even karmic nature can outwork in ways that may at the outset seem confusing or counterproductive to our desires; ultimately though, when the clearance is complete, a brighter day dawns. As another proverb says, '*A foul morning may turn to a fair day.*'

Linked with this proverb is the spirit of generosity and labour in the form of the busy Bee. It symbolises the tireless worker who by day ceaselessly labours and gives so freely to the hive of the collective whole. You are reminded that it is by working for the good of others, by your generosity and effort that you in turn will receive. At present you may not see the silver lining that you are sowing, but like the new growth in nature many things remain hidden until their time to flower arrives.

There is a time to be born and a time to move-on, a time to evaluate and learn, until the circle once again completes its turn, and a new birth follows. All serves a purpose and nothing is truly lost, only transformed, enriched and glorified by the experience. As you have given (generously?) you shall receive.

4 & 1

Where there is a Will,
There is a Way

The Lion - The Spirit of Power
with Knowledge

This proverb indicates that whatever you have in mind can be achieved, even if plenty of willpower has to be exerted. Making this is a call for determination. It says, go ahead, draw-up a plan and follow it through. There will be obstacles, problems to overcome, possible setbacks, but if you have the willpower you will succeed. Another proverb says, '*Knowledge is power,*' so you are encouraged to use your knowledge wisely in the execution of your will.

Associated with this proverb is the spirit of power with knowledge in the form of the Lion. The Lion symbolises royalty, the king of the jungle, bestowing strength with protection. With the power of the king in your corner you may chase your dreams with renewed confidence, trusting in your own inner power. Do not be afraid if called upon to act as leader, simply follow your visions and have the courage to speak the truth.

Life itself was never meant to be a struggle. The struggles we have are so often not truly with others or the world, but with ourselves. The strong will of the directing spirit so often struggles with the weakness of the physical mind and emotions. We are swayed by comfort at the expense of global commonsense. Those who can engage their higher self will and acknowledge their gifts can achieve their ambitions.

Those Who Would Climb the Ladder Must Begin At the Bottom

The Turtle - The Spirit of Shyness and Timidity

Patience is the keyword here. This proverb teaches that each step upon the pathway of happiness, success, or achievement must be taken with care and precision. You cannot rush in this matter. Take one day at a time to develop and make good your progression. Then, surely then, you will ascend to the heights of your expectations. As another proverb says, '*Step after step the ladder is ascended,*' spiritually-the rungs on the ladder are the experiences of life.

The Turtle, the spirit of shyness and timidity, is associated with this proverb. These are not undesirable weaknesses, but inner qualities of one who understands that life is eternal and that the ladder extends to heights beyond our comprehension. Externally if one chooses to they can still retain a hard shell, to protect from the knocks of life, while inwardly, they can be themselves.

Evolution itself is subject to the truth of this poignant proverb. As the flower becomes the bird or fish that in turn becomes the animal that eventually ascends as its soul transmigrates into the individuality of human form. In between, innumerable small steps of progression are taken in the (mostly unconscious) quest for ascension, from one level of attainment to the next.

4 & 3

The Early Bird Catches the Worm

The Lark - The Spirit of Renewal

This proverb counsels a quick response to a situation; otherwise you may well miss out. You may need to be brave, to summon from within the inner-strength and courage to go ahead, for this may put you upon a new pathway, but your inner desire should not be repressed. There are issues in life that some delay, even deny, sometimes year in year out, which ultimately must be faced. Many fears are cultivated by a reluctance to go forward and face a subject or situation head on. Yet once faced its power diminishes significantly leaving one perplexed as to why it was ever held in foreboding. Another proverb you may wish to remember says, *'Time waits for no one.'*

The spirit of renewal in the form of the Lark is linked with this proverb. It symbolises the dawning of a new day, adventure and commitment. The Lark gives us an early wake up call encouraging us not to miss the first worm or opportunity of the day. It sings to attract a mate or to proclaim its territory, as it goes forward with renewed cheer. Each day is new, a fresh start to life or to whatever we wish it to be. To avoid later regrets, one should always endeavour to take the chances that life offers.

In the physical sense everything has a start and an end. Spiritually there is no end, only the end of a new beginning, and a renewal of life upon another pathway. The pendulum swings right and then left as it seeks to find a balance. Those who can master negative impulses yet remain calm and centred, find the rhythm of life that brings constant renewal to their spirit.

4 & 4

Fortune Favours the Brave

The Panther - The Spirit of Protection

Often there comes a time when to move forward with a desire one has to take a deep breath and proceed, even if it is necessary to move into uncharted territory. This proverb reminds us that such acts of bravery often produce rewards, and they can come in abundance. One certainty is that those who allow fear to deter them will never receive the blessing of the available good fortune, whether physical, emotional, mental or spiritual in nature. So you are counselled to go forward and be of good cheer and, as another proverb says, '*When fortune smiles, embrace her.*'

Linked with this proverb is the Panther, the spirit of protection. This beautiful sleek big black cat will be your guardian animal at this time. Symbolically in certain situations he (or she) is also said to represent the warrior under whose guardianship victory is assured; the proverb, '*Better to die with honour than live with shame,*' could be his motto.

It takes courage to step into the unknown, to go boldly where many fear to tread. Yet we are all braver than many realise, for what else brings us into this incarnation other than the free-will desire of our own spirit to progress, experience, learn and serve? At all times we can call upon The Power, The Source, for protection and for guidance.

4 & 5

If It Were Not For Hope, the Heart Would Break

The Swan - The Spirit of Dreams

This proverb calls for hope, encouraging you to keep going no matter how demanding or testing your current situation or circumstance. Something may well be weighing heavily upon your heart, making you weary, but always there is hope and a way forward. As another proverb says, *'Humble hearts have humble desires,'* yet, no concern, problem or obstacle is ever presented to you that you cannot rise above, solve or overcome. Expectations can be fulfilled, hang on to your dreams and trust.

Associated with this proverb is the spirit of dreams in the form of the graceful Swan. Symbolically this says, keep dreaming, and enjoy your dreams, for they may just come true. This can also indicate partnerships, particularly of an emotional or spiritual nature (friends, guides or The Great Spirit). When the Swan glides over the smooth waters it indicates that all is or will be well. Rough waters indicate that things are yet to settle and will need time to resolve. In which way do you see the waters in your mind?

Hope is a virtue that helps to inspire and drive us all forward. If it were not for the hope of progression and advancement or for contributing or making good, we would never incarnate again and again as we do. This shows us that hope and expectation live on in spirit as it may do upon earth. The heart also plays its part, for when it aches it is telling us so much about our true desires and motives. Without its guidance hope would indeed be more difficult to sustain.

4 & 6

What Goes Around Comes Around

The Butterfly – The Spirit of Balance and Attraction

This proverb tells us that all receive what may be deemed *rewards* or *retribution* according to their own making. If it is you who needs the warning this urges you to say or do only what is right, fair and just, or to hold your own counsel. Otherwise you may have cause for regret. If it concerns another, know that all will reap their own just deserts. It may be wise to stand back and take no action, remember, '*Patience is a virtue,*' and that in time all will balance justly.

The Butterfly, symbolising the spirit of balance and attraction, is associated with this proverb. Having come from the chrysalis it can also signify a transformation complete. It encourages you to give, as you would like to receive. It embraces within itself the yin and the yang, the two halves of the psyche, also known as the negative and the positive or the feminine and the masculine. Its two wings reflect mirror images of its balanced beauty.

Cosmically, this proverb reflects the great spiritual-universal law of cause and effect. All is registered in the very vibrations of our own being, our spirit. Love brings love, kindness brings kindness, and compassion brings compassion in the full karmic circle of life. Whereas, all negative actions, thoughts and responses draw their like. In this unfailing way we truly do attract and control our own destiny.

5 & 1

It Is In Vain To Cast Your Net Where There Is No Fish

The Whale - The Spirit of Understanding

This proverb indicates that you may be seeking something that is unavailable. We all have wishes and desires but if it is not there for you, even if only at this moment in time, you may need to look in another direction. Another proverb says, '*There is a time for all things,*' and what is missing in one area may be in abundance elsewhere.

The spirit of understanding in the form of the majestic Whale is linked with this proverb. This can indicate that deep emotions are involved; forgiveness of self and others is a virtue that when embraced brings advancement to the soul. If you can visualise a calm sea your emotions will also settle. From your present situation you can gain greater understanding of life and, perhaps of greater significance and value, of *yourself*.

Sometimes it is easier to have faith and trust all that comes your way in life. To be truly wise it becomes necessary to fully understand what lies beneath and goes to make the fabric and structures in all aspects of life. It also becomes necessary to seek within, to discover the core spirit of your own being, to unpeel the layers of indoctrination imposed by society and life experiences to reveal the real you, the being of love.

5 & 2

In For A Penny, In For A Pound

The Cat - The Spirit of Independence

This proverb suggests that your concern, whatever it is, needs full commitment. In the past you may have given it plenty of thought, yet if you wish to go forward the time has come when you need to invest wholeheartedly. It is likely that you already know the pathway; this proverb encourages you to follow it. For only in this way will you do justice to others, an idea, or to yourself. There is another proverb that says, '*One reason is as good as fifty*,' that you may wish to consider.

Linked with this proverb is the Cat, symbolising the spirit of independence. This signifies plenty of movement and investigation, while plenty of moments for rest and recuperation should be reserved. You may not wish to be tied down by routine or commitments that do not suit your personality or desires, although sometimes it is these that ground us and stop us from roaming too far for our own good. So this says enjoy the diversities of life, independence with commitment, moments for all that is in your life, and moments for curling-up and simply doing nothing, for in this way you can enjoy the best of all worlds.

Spiritually, many people pay their dues and remain a spectator. The *prize* goes to the one who is willing to stand up to be counted. To the one who takes responsibility for their actions and shows full commitment and respect to their inner-knowledge and soul ambition.

5 & 3

A Bird in the Hand Is Worth Two in the Bush

The Eagle - The Spirit of Vision and Foresight

This proverb indicates that now might be a time to count your blessings and be grateful for what you have rather than reflect on what you do not have. We all have gains and we all have losses, pluses and minuses, in and at all levels of life. This can be a call to settle for the obvious, even the practical, what is in front of you, and not to live in the fantasy or dream world of make-believe. This world of course has its place, but not beyond commonsense and good reason. As another proverb says, '*There is a time to wink as well as to see.*'

Associated with this proverb is the spirit of vision and foresight in the form of the Eagle. Signals are sent to us from all dimensions, they are transmitted but are we sensitive enough to concisely receive them? They will not always advise changes. Just as frequently they may say, *you already have all the necessary qualities, cultivate them, and you will find success, satisfaction and contentment.*

In life judgement and self-examination of motive is at all times called for, if rarely adhered to! Should you be satisfied with what you already possess, that which could be nurtured to ensure its growth, or should you seek that which is currently out of reach or hidden from your view? Whichever pathways we choose to follow justice will always prevail, so whatever you deserve you ultimately will receive.

5 & 4

If The Blind Lead the Blind Both Shall Fall Into the Ditch

The Donkey - The Spirit of Illusion

The message this proverb sends is that you need to take a closer look at your own direction and possibly that of another, depending upon whether you consider yourself the one doing the leading or the one being led. This may also be a call to *open your eyes* to a person, situation, even an organisation that is not serving you well. You may need to bear in mind another proverb which says, '*Affection blinds reason.*' For it is only by opening ones eyes to see the light that we realise change is required and is perhaps very necessary. So this could be a call to see beyond the illusions of life and to allow a new and brighter day to dawn.

The Donkey, symbolising the spirit of illusion, is associated with this proverb. The Donkey sees the carrot and pursues it blind to the fact that as always, it hangs permanently just out of reach. You are called upon to see beyond the illusions, so that you may follow your true pathway without falling into any ditches. At the same time you may need to practise non-interference, to allow others to make their own choices for better or worse, for in this way they too will learn.

We should not seek to judge, for who knows what in past incarnations we may have done? What can be said is that in many ways throughout history, particularly religious history, in vast numbers, the blind have led the blind, and fallen into misunderstanding, hatred and suppression. It takes courage and fortitude to climb out, to gain your own clear and better view, so that one can see the light of reason and gain a fuller understanding of the simplistic beauty that life offers.

5 & 5

You May Lead a Horse to the Water, but You Cannot Make Him Drink

The Horse - The Spirit of Freedom

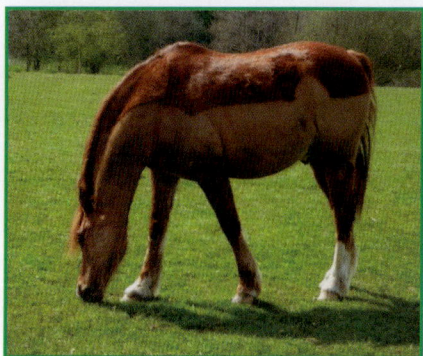

This proverb asks you to stand back from a situation (or person) and let prevail whatever will be. Those taken to the waters edge often need time to absorb, so you may have to show patience. Another proverb says, *'None so deaf as those who will not hear.'* Stubborn emotions may be involved and, particularly for those who love total freedom, these can take time to settle.

The spirit of freedom in the form of the Horse is linked with this proverb. A Horse may also indicate a journey, leading to communication, a reunion or a new encounter. This should be on your own terms, and not something thrust upon you, otherwise you may feel pressured and need to dig your heels in and stick to your own devices.

It is difficult to come to a realisation or learn anything overnight; particularly anything involved or of greater significance, since patience to mentally absorb new ideas is generally required. Expansion and dawning of greater awareness comes slowly, like the pebble upon the beach washed by water, the mind ever so gradually is bathed by the incoming and outgoing tides of thought, before the gemstone within can be revealed.

Many a True Word Is Spoken In Jest

The Coyote — The Spirit of Mischief and Trickery

This proverb could be advising you that others think less of you than you might have expected. But on the other side of the coin, others might hold you in higher esteem than you realise or hold yourself. So this proverb might also be advising you to pay greater attention to others, to listen to what they have to say; while it may also be advising you to listen to the unspoken word; the jest (or laughter–genuine, false or nervous), so that you might see behind the mask. It may also be suggesting that your true feelings might for better or for worse be exposed in this way. For as another proverb says, '*What the heart thinks, the tongue speaks.*'

Linked with this proverb is the Coyote, symbolising the spirit of mischief and trickery. It can also indicate constraint, as life plays its tricks, causing pain and confusion, as many are mischief-makers. But with the Coyote in your corner, you should become more aware and able to separate the truth from the jest, to see beyond the spoken word.

Behind the mask of ego lies the jester within the spirit of life. For at our core the spirit delights in humour. The true self holds no illusions of pious self-righteousness, as projected at their congregations by old-fashioned preachers. So this may also be a call for you to release the humour within, and not to involve yourself in the absurdity of taking this short life too seriously. In so doing, you may release the spirit of your true inner self, that which holds much joy and love.

6 & 1

*Those Who Desire Honour,
Are Not Worthy Of Honour*

*The Zebra - The Spirit of
Clarity*

This proverb suggests that someone around you thinks very highly of him or herself and wishes others to do likewise. You are counselled not to be gullible enough to fall under their spell, but to clearly see through the projected image of the ego to the true person, and under clear scrutiny you will most likely find them wanting and unworthy. There is another proverb that may prove useful to consider, it says, *'Beauty is but skin-deep.'*

Associated with this proverb is the spirit of clarity in the form of the Zebra. This symbolises a need to see things clearly, in black and white. It urges you not to allow others to colour or cloud your vision, for if you do so you could be misled. Visualise this image as you sit in quiet contemplation or meditation and seek clarity, in so doing you may find the truth and know who to trust and which pathway to follow. This could be an important crossroads in your life.

In spiritual terms it is not always wise to be a pacifist or accept everything at face value. There are many occasions when one truly should respond to the challenge of those who would have us passively follow the herd. The spirit should not be caged or penned, it is free, no one other than the individual themselves holds authority over it. To honour and respect your own being is a birthright, never let others lead you where you do not wish to go or to dominate your free will; develop the capacity to clearly see the motive behind the agenda.

6 & 2

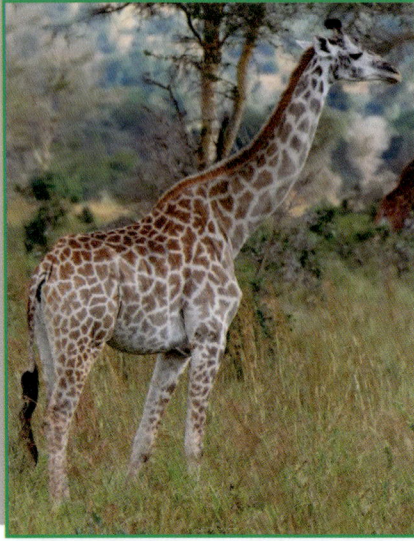

To Get To the Fruit of the Tree, You Sometimes Have To Go Out On a Limb

The Giraffe - The Spirit of Grace

This proverb encourages you to be bold, and to be willing to take a risk; for there are times when it is necessary to go out on a limb, to risk loss or embarrassment. Metaphorically the tree branch can always break, but on the other hand it may hold firm, and you will reach what you seek. While if you do nothing, risk nothing, you will most certainly gain nothing. As another proverb says, '*If the mountain will not come to Mahomet, Mahomet must go to the mountain.*' In other words at very least make an attempt to reach, find or get what you seek.

The spirit of grace in the form of the elegant Giraffe is associated with this proverb. Symbolically this suggests that which you seek, your higher aspirations in particular, is within your reach. The neck of the Giraffe evolved long to reach the succulent new shoots in the higher branches at the top of tree, you may need to stretch, but that which you desire will be within your reach.

No experience in life is ever wasted. Not all conclude the way in which we might consciously desire, if so life would be too easy, it would lack challenge, and become somewhat boring. We would effectively gain nothing, for how could we truly appreciate our successes, if failure was never a possibility? To forever reach for higher targets, greater achievements, to identify and work on weaknesses, is the hallmark of an aspiring spirit.

6 & 3

Liberty Is Worth More than Gold

The Crow - The Spirit of Justice

This proverb hits home on multiple levels for everyone. Freedom of thought, of expression, the liberty to be the person you choose to be (with just respect for others) is paramount. It is a spiritual right. Has your liberty been suppressed in any way? If so, it is a call to reclaim it. To stand-up for your rights and for what is fair, reasonable and just. You are worth more than material pursuits. Is it time to exert your will, to reclaim your life? Another proverb says, '*Honesty is the best policy*,' and honesty to the inner spirit, that which through intuition and conscience guides us in the right direction, is particularly of great importance.

The Crow, symbolising the spirit of justice is linked with this proverb. This can also indicate a need to be aware of law and order, to remain disciplined. There are also higher laws, the laws of spirit. For instance, what you give out you will receive back, liberty and justice included. Integrity of character is a virtue worth cherishing.

Without just cause we should never usurp the liberty of another, and you should always hold your own liberty dear. Gold is of the earth, a transient material wealth, liberty is of the spirit, and spirit is eternal. Those pure in heart will eventually reap a higher and purer justice. For in time the scales will always be balanced.

6 & 4

Fate Leads the Willing, but Drives the Stubborn

The Bear - The Spirit of Courage and Willpower

This proverb tells you that you have two choices, to willingly follow the direction of the inner spirit or to resist. The choice is your own, but on some level of your being you probably are aware that your path is set. Why struggle against your destiny? As another proverb says, *'Those who will not go over the stile must be thrust through the gate.'* If you can willingly follow your instincts your pathway will be smoother and more fulfilling.

Linked with this proverb is the spirit of courage and willpower in the form of the Bear. This, when visualised, will give you greater strength, the power and determination to achieve on any level that presents itself to you. It will enhance and stimulate your own willpower, and encourage you to find the pathway that best suits you at this moment in time.

Spiritually the bells ring out loud and clear, but only those who are willing to listen hear the chimes. Upon this Earth there is something like six billion people and by far the greater majority are spiritually deaf. Many adhere to a religion, but none of these has the answers that the truly open-minded seeker craves. Belief can never match knowledge, truth and ultimately wisdom, which comes to those who have the courage to personally investigate.

6 & 5

They Who Dance, Are Thought Mad By Those Who Hear Not The Music

The Buffalo - The Spirit of Strength

This proverb urges you to follow (or continue to follow) a pathway that the inner-self craves. Others may think you mad, for it is a tuning fork call that few hear, and with which even fewer respond to harmonise. Their failure to respond to the music of the soul should not deter you. Those who have an inner quality, perhaps even a specific ability, should always use it. A further proverb that may prove useful to remember is, *'Truth will come to light.'*

Associated with this proverb is the Buffalo, symbolising the spirit of strength. When visualised, this can fortify you against the many people who understand little and readily ridicule those who seek to follow the pathway of inner direction. A sense of wholeness can come to those who follow the inner calling, and satisfaction that surpasses the everyday successes of material physical reality.

The beat of life says, *Dance away*, every now and again the rhythm or tune of the music may change, but there is no reason why we cannot all be open, receptive and responsive to its change. We need only adjust our own rhythm, as nature adjusts her rhythm, to keep in step and reap the pleasures that harmony with the beat of life brings. The wise student who sits in meditation or quiet contemplation, if they allow their thoughts to drift in the right direction, will feel this beat as surely as they may hear their own heart beat.

6 & 6

Everyone Loves a Good Mystery

The Raven - The Spirit of Secrets, Mystery and Initiation

If your life seems like a mystery do not despair, it is intended that way. The pathways you take are your own choice, they may on occasions lead you away from your lessons but life is a circle, so you will soon find yourself back on the right pathway. This proverb says, enjoy the mysteries that life offers, they are part of the experience. While another proverb says, '*Truth is stranger than fiction*,' so expect many surprises along the way.

The spirit of secrets, mystery and initiation in the form of the Raven is associated with this proverb. The Raven is also known as the trickster, yet is valued as wise in oracles and omens. He (or she) is also considered a *messenger and watcher of the gods*. Visualise upon this beautiful jet-black bird as you await your own initiation into…well, that is a mystery for you to reveal.

The biggest mystery as far as most people are concerned is the meaning of life. Yet it is so simple, it is soul evolution. Earth (or any other inhabited planet) is used for incarnations, which are form stepping-stones that allow for soul growth or unfoldment. As we progress we can use form after form to learn lessons through experiences. A final proverb for you to ponder says, '*Those who will enter into paradise must have a good key*.' The key is wisdom gained through experience!

Printed in Great Britain
by Amazon.co.uk, Ltd.,
Marston Gate.